SandCastle™

Primeros Sonidos

Chela y Chuy

Cathy Camarena, M.Ed., and Gloria B. Ruff, M.Ed.

Consulting Editors

Lourdes Flores-Hanson, M.S.E., and Gloria Rosso-White

ABDO Publishing Company

capstone

www.capstoneclassroom.com

Credits
Curriculum Coordinator: Nancy Tuminelly
Cover and Interior Design and Production: Mighty Media
Child Photography: Steven Wewerka, Wewerka Photography
Photo Credits: AbleStock, Brand X Pictures, Photodisc

ISBN 978-1-4966-0325-8 (paperback)

Printed in the United States of America.
874

SandCastle™ books are created by a professional team of educators, reading specialists, and content developers around five essential components that include phonemic awareness, phonics, vocabulary, text comprehension, and fluency. All books are written, reviewed, and leveled for guided and early intervention reading, and designed for use in shared, guided, and independent reading and writing activities to support a balanced approach to literacy instruction.

SandCastle Level: Beginning

ch

ABCChDEFGH
IJKLLLMNÑOP
QRSTUVWXYZ

abcchdefgh
ijklllmnñop
qrstuvwxyz

Chela

Chuy

chivo

chaleco

chile

chocolate

chico

Vemos el  .

Vemos el  .

Vemos el  .

Vemos el .

Vemos el .

Chuy tiene un chivo.
El chivo es gris.

Chela tiene
mucho chocolate.

Chela come el
chocolate.

¡Al chivo le gusta el chocolate!

¿Cuáles de estas cosas comienzan con ch?

Más palabras que comienzan con **ch**

champú

charco

cheque

chicle

choza

About SandCastle™

A professional team of educators, reading specialists, and content developers created the SandCastle™ series to support young readers as they develop reading skills and strategies and increase their general knowledge. The SandCastle™ series has four levels that correspond to early literacy development in young children. The levels are provided to help teachers and parents select the appropriate books for young readers.

Emerging Readers
(no flags)

Beginning Readers
(1 flag)

Transitional Readers
(2 flags)

Fluent Readers
(3 flags)

These levels are meant only as a guide. All levels are subject to change.

ABDO Publishing Company

www.abdopub.com

capstone®

www.capstoneclassroom.com